Step by Step
Sri Lankan Cookery

Published by
Vijitha Yapa Publications

Step by Step
Sri Lankan Cookery

Manel Ratnatunga

A Vijitha Yapa Paperback

Vijitha Yapa Publications
Unity Plaza 2, Galle Road, Colombo 4, Sri Lanka
Tel : (94 1) 596960 Fax : (94 1) 584801
e-mail : vijiyapa@sri.lanka.net

First Published February 2002
First Reprint - January 2003
Second Reprint - June 2003
Third Reprint - Oct 2003
Fourth Reprint - May 2004
Reprint August 2005

ISBN 955 8095 12 5

PRINTED IN INDIA

Preface

Sri Lanka is the land of paddy fields, coconut and palmyra trees and is surrounded by the sea on all sides. Therefore, people eat varieties of rice and curries prepared in coconut milk accompanied with fish as part of their daily diet. Green leaves made into mellums are a daily must. Dessert usually is curd laced with treacle from the Kitul tree.

The Dutch introduced kokis, lovecake and lampries. The British westernised Sri Lankan palates. Today Indian food is a great favourite. But our own food is still the best for us as a daily routine.

I thank Subhadra Amarasekera, Verona Samarasekera, Lakshmi Perera, Anoja Wijesundera and Rani Ranasinghe for their loving help.

H.E. Mangala Moonesinghe and his wife Gnana did the photographs for this book at the Sri Lankan High Commission in Delhi. My heartfelt thanks to both of them.

Manel Ratnatunga

Food Values

Coconut
- Is an elixir of life. Coconut oil is a neutral oil. It neither increases nor decreases the serum cholesterol level. It absorbs vitamin A. Coconut fat is used in many imported milk food for infants, gives energy to vegetarians and detoxifies toxic food.

Curry leaves
- Another elixir. Good for blood pressure.

Fenugreek
- Rich in phosphate, calcium and iron. Good for flatulence and onset of diarrhoea.

Fish
- Vitamin B, vitamin D and calcium in the bones of small fish. Controls pressure.

Garlic
- Lowers cholesterol, aids digestion and soothes upset stomach.

Ginger
- Soothes upset stomach and prevents colic.

Goraka
- Helps digestion and prevents allergic reactions. Traditionally used to preserve red fish which could cause allergic reactions.

Jaggery
- Provides energy and aids digestion.

Spices
- Aids digestion, like cloves and cardamoms.

Unpolished rice
- Rich in iron, calcium and fibre.

All herbs, leaves, ginger and garlic to be used in the recipes should be fresh

Approximate Conversion Table

1 lb	= 450 gms	1 pint	= 568 ml
8 oz	= 225 gms	1/2 pint	= 284 ml
4 oz	= 125 gms	1/4 pint	= 142 ml
1 oz	= 15 gms	1 3/4 pint	= 1 litre (approx.)

Abbreviations used:

Teaspoon — t
Tablespoon — T
Cup — c

Glossary

Sri Lankan	English	Sri Lankan	English
batala	a variety of yam	kos	jakfruit
billing	an acid fruit	kurakkan	a type of millet
blood fish	any fish with red flesh (tuna, bream, mullet, etc.)	maduru	sweet cumin seed
		Maldive fish	a variety of tuna fish, smoked and dried.
cadjunut	cashewnut	manioc	yam
ekel	hard spine of a coconut leaf	mellun	cooked green leaves used as a substitute for salad
goraka	brindle berry	mukunuwenna	a variety of local leaf
gotukola	a green leaf	polos	tender jakfruit
hathavariya	a variety of local leaf	rampa	a fragrant leaf, like bayleaf.
innala	a local vegetable		
jambu	pink fruit	rasa kavili	sweets
karavila	bitter gourd	siyambala	tamarind
kathuru murunga	the leaf from the kathuru murunga tree	suduru	cumin seed
		thibbatu	a local vegetable
kehel muwa	plantain flower	vattakka	yellow pumpkin
kohila	a local vegetable	white fish	like seer and para
kokis	cookie or Dutch koekjes		

Contents

CURRY POWDER

Simple Curry Powder

INGREDIENTS

1/2 lb coriander seeds
2 oz cinnamon
2 oz cumin seeds
1 oz sweet cumin seeds
2 oz rampa
3 sprigs of curry leaves
1 oz raw rice
3 cardamoms
6 cloves

METHOD

1. Grind separately, then mix together. Cloves and cardamoms can be ground together. Store in an airtight bottle.

9

Kiri Bath (Milk Rice)

Serves 4

INGREDIENTS

6 oz scraped coconut

✻

8 oz raw rice (not boiled rice)
1 t salt

✻

METHOD

1. Squeeze the coconut to get 1 cup of thick milk. Cow milk can be used but coconut gives the real flavour.

✻

2. Boil the rice as usual with water. When almost done, add the coconut milk and salt. Stir well. Simmer till done. Spoon onto a flat dish. Smoothen the top. When cool, cut into diagonals or squares.

✻

Kiri bath takes pride of place on the Sri Lankan table. At all auspicious ceremonies, personal, business or governance, one is served kiri bath milk rice. It is eaten with chilli sambol and a banana.

Roti

INGREDIENTS

2 c wheat flour
1 1/4 t salt
4 T margarine
2 c scraped coconut
water
a board and a roller

❋

a flat pan

❋

1 red onion, chopped
1-2 green chilli, chopped
grated Maldive fish

❋

METHOD

1. Mix the flour, salt and margarine. Add the scraped coconut. Moisten into a soft dough with water. Knead a bit.
Form four balls and roll out on a board. Two pieces of wax paper under and on top of the roti will save the trouble of having to wash both the board as well as the roller.

❋

2. Cook on a flat pan on a moderate fire. When the underside is done, turn over. It will have a mottled appearance.

❋

3. Optional: One could add a sprinkling of chopped red onion, chopped green chilli and a dash of grated Maldive fish to enrich the flavour.

❋

Roti can be made with roasted rice flour or wheat flour.
Traditional accompaniment is chilli sambol or any curry with thick gravy.

Kola Kenda (Conjee of Leaves)

INGREDIENTS

1 coconut
3 oz gotukola
3 oz hathavariya
3 oz mukunuwenna
✻
4 oz raw rice (unboiled)
salt to taste

✻

METHOD

1. Scrape a full coconut. Put it, with the leaves, into a mortar and pound it to extract the juice.

✻

2. Boil the rice. When mushy, add the juice extracted from the pounded leaves. When it comes to a boil twice, it is ready. Add salt to taste.

✻

This 'porridge' was given by the state to school children during President Premadasa's time. It was a breakfast food, even in the homes of the elite before the introduction of bacon and eggs.

Note : Gotukola by itself, or gotukola and one other kind of leaf can be used.

Yams

Batala and manioc are favourite yams for breakfast. Boil the yams. Add salt. Eat with scraped coconut or chilli sambol.

The Sri Lankan manioc needs care. It contains cyanide, so any manioc that has a damaged skin, exposed to the elements is not eaten. Only the newly uprooted ones are consumed. The rough bark is discarded, and the flesh is boiled with the lid open. One never eats anything with it that contains ginger. Scraped coconut which detoxifies it, and some chilli sambol are the traditional accompaniments.

Yellow Rice with Coconut Milk

Serves 4-5

INGREDIENTS

1 lb rice

✳

1 T ghee/margarine / butter
2" rampa
2" lemon-grass
a few curry leaves
1/2 Bombay onion /6 red onions

✳

extracted milk of 1/2 a coconut
(There can be the first, second and
third extracts to produce enough
liquid)
1/2 T Maldive fish (optional)
3 cloves
6 pepper seeds
1/4 t turmeric powder
2 t salt

✳

4 cardamoms, split into two each

✳

lightly fried sultanas, nuts, onion
slivers, hard-boiled egg halves or
whatever is handy

✳

METHOD

1. Wash and drain the rice if necessary.

   ✳

2. Heat ghee and saute the herbs and onion till the onion is light brown in colour. Add the rice and stir well for 3 minutes.

   ✳

3. Add the coconut milk and the other ingredients. There must be sufficient liquid for the rice to cook.

   ✳

4. Cook till three-quarters of the liquid has been evaporated. Add the cardamoms.

   ✳

5. Garnish with all, or any one, or not at all.

   ✳

Vegetable Pillau

Serves 4

INGREDIENTS

1 lb rice
1 stock cube
4 cardamoms
4 cloves
1" piece cinnamon
water

✳

3 cloves of garlic
1" piece ginger

✳

4 oz carrot
4 oz cabbage
4 oz leeks
2 green chillies

✳

2 T ghee,
4 oz onions
1" rampa
1" lemon-grass,
a few curry leaves

✳

*(12 oz vegetables and green chillies
as mentioned above in step 3)*

✳

METHOD

1. Boil the rice with the stock cube and spices.

✳

2. Chop and keep aside.

✳

3. Shred the vegetables.

✳

4. Heat ghee. Fry the onions and herbs till the onions are golden brown.

✳

5. Add the prepared vegetables.

✳

Contd...

1 1/2 t curry powder,
garlic and ginger, chopped (as in step 2)
1/2 t pepper
1 t khas-khas
1 t chilli powder
1/2 t saffron
1 t salt

✳

5 T ketchup
1/2 t rose essence

✳

6. Add the listed ingredients.

✳

7. Add the rice, ketchup and rose essence and mix well.

✳

Vegetable Fried Rice

Vegetable Fried Rice

Serves 8-10

INGREDIENTS

500 gms basmati or samba

❋

1 big onion
4 gms butter
3" rampa
3" lemon-grass
12 curry leaves

❋

50 gms diced beans
100 gms shredded carrots
50 gms shredded cabbage
100 gms chopped leeks
1 T water

❋

3-4 crushed cardamoms
50 gms raisins or sultanas
salt to taste

❋

METHOD

1. Cook the rice

❋

2. Fry the onion in butter or margarine. Then add the herbs and stir for a minute.

❋

3. Add and cover with a lid. Cook on a low flame till the vegetables are tender.

❋

4. Mix well

❋

Non-vegetarian Fried Rice

INGREDIENTS

500 gms chicken or lean mutton, cut into small pieces.

✳

100 gms butter or margarine
2" rampa
3" lemon-grass
12 curry leaves
100 gms sliced onions

✳

1 kilo basmati or samba

✳

meat as above
2" piece cinnamon
6 cloves
a pinch of saffron
salt to taste
6 powdered cardamoms
100 gms shredded carrots
100 gms shredded leeks

✳

METHOD

Serves 8

1. Put the chicken or mutton in a pan and boil in water (enough to cover the meat). Simmer and cook, but do not overcook.

✳

2. Melt butter and add the herbs and onions. Fry till the onions are lightly brown.

✳

3. Add the meat pieces and spices to the rice. Add all the water in which the meat was boiled. Add more boiling water if needed to cook the rice. Stir well.

✳

4. When the rice is half-cooked, add the mentioned ingredients, cover and cook on a low flame till the rice is done. Stir well before serving.

✳

Lampries (Rice Parcels in Banana Leaves)

Serves 4

INGREDIENTS

1 lb rice
enough meat stock or stock cubes to
boil the rice

2 oz ghee
5 red onions, sliced
2" rampa and lemon-grass
a few curry leaves

2" piece cinnamon
8 peppercorns
3 cloves, crushed
salt to taste

5 cardamoms, crushed

✳

METHOD

1. Wash and drain the rice. Make meat
   stock or use stock cubes.

✳

2. Heat ghee. Fry the onions and leaves till
   the onions are golden brown.

3. Add the drained rice and stir well. Add
   sufficient stock to cook the rice. Add the
   cinnamon, peppercorns and cloves. Add
   salt.

4. Cook till the rice is three-fourth done.
   Add the cardamoms and cook till the rice
   is fully done. Pack as shown in the next
   recipe.

✳

This was a Dutch legacy, now a Sri Lankan speciality.

How to pack Lampries

INGREDIENTS	METHOD
cut banana leaves into 14"x12" (or aluminium foil)	1. Wash the banana leaves. Warm them over the fire. Brush the inner side of the leaves with the coconut milk.
✴	✴
cooked rice *a little coconut milk*	2. Spoon a cupful of the rice on each leaf. Sprinkle with a little coconut milk.
✴	✴
chicken curry *fried plantain curry* *cutlet balls* *blachan sambol* *onion sambol*	3. Put 2 T of each curry around the rice on the leaves. Fold into parcels and hold with a toothpick. (traditionally with an ekel). Warm in an oven at 350°F for 20 minutes. Remove the banana leaf and serve.
✴	✴

This is cooked in a banana leaf to add to the flavour.
Options: Fried bringal curry and seeni sambol can also be used.

GRAVIES

Kiri Hodhi (Coconut Milk Gravy)

INGREDIENTS

1 t chopped onion
1" rampa and lemon-grass
a small sprig of curry leaves
1" piece cinnamon
1/8 t fenugreek
1 t coriander seeds
1/4 t cumin seeds
1/4 t sweet cumin seeds
1 clove of garlic, chopped
1/4" piece ginger, chopped
1/2 t salt (check taste)
a pinch of saffron
1/4 t Maldive fish (optional)
1/2 c water

❈

3/4 c coconut milk.
juice of 1/4 lime

❈

METHOD

1. Put all the listed ingredients into a saucepan with water and boil till it is cooked.

❈

2. Add the coconut milk and lime juice. Stir well or it will curdle. Remove from the fire.

❈

Children begin to eat curries with this gravy right from when they are in nursery. It remains a favourite till the end of their lives.

Thambun Hodhi

INGREDIENTS

6 large cloves of garlic

6 red onions
a sprig of curry leaves
1 t cumin seeds
1 t sweet cumin seeds
1 goraka
1/2 t fenugreek
2 t coriander seeds
5 peppercorns
1" rampa
2" piece cinnamon
3 cloves of garlic

❉

3 cloves of garlic
3 c water
salt to taste

❉

METHOD

1. Clean the garlic and keep aside.

   ❉

2. Crush together the listed ingredients for best results, or simply assemble all in a saucepan.

   ❉

3. Add water and the remaining garlic cut into pieces. Boil and reduce to 1 1/2 cups. Strain and add salt to taste. Serve with the garlic pieces to consume them.

   ❉

If you feel slightly seedy, without an appetite or even with an upset stomach, this broth will be welcomed by your stomach.

Fish Moligatanni

INGREDIENTS

1 tomato
8 oz fish with bone
1 pint water

1 T ghee / margarine
1 Bombay onion
about 10 curry leaves
1 T curry powder
1/2 t cumin seeds
1/2 t sweet cumin seeds
a pinch of saffron
1/4 t fenugreek

1 pint fish stock with fish pieces.
(remove bones)
3/4 t salt
1/4 pint coconut milk
a squeeze of lime

METHOD

1. Blanch the tomato and blend it in a food processor to make a puree. Then add the puree into the fish. Pressure cook to make the fish stock.

2. Heat ghee in a saucepan. Temper the onion, leaves and spices.

3. Add the stock, salt, milk and lime juice.

Vegetarian Moligatanni

INGREDIENTS

2 T butter / oil
2 Bombay onions, chopped
4 cloves of garlic, chopped
2 carrots, diced
1 stalk celery, chopped
1 large potato, diced
1 medium leek, sliced

❋

1 T curry powder
1 T flour
1 1/2 pint stock made with 2-3
    vegetable soup cubes.

❋

1 tomato, diced
1 T sugar
1 T sultanas
2 oz almonds
a few peppercorns
1 c coconut milk
salt to taste

❋

coriander leaves

❋

METHOD

1. Fry the onions and garlic till they are slightly brown. Stir in the vegetables. Cook for five minutes.

❋

2. Stir in the curry powder and flour. Gradually add the stock and bring to a boil.

❋

3. Add the rest of the ingredients. Simmer for half an hour.

❋

4. Blend the soup in a liquidiser until smooth. Reheat before use. Check seasoning. Garnish with coriander leaves.

❋

Excellent with string hoppers

Chilli Sauce (for fried fish)

INGREDIENTS

1/2 oz chilli powder
1 oz mustard seeds
1/2" piece ginger
4 cloves of garlic
1/2 c artificial vinegar
3 oz sugar
salt to taste

❋

1 t cornflour or wheatflour
tepid water

❋

❋

fried fish
a few red onions
a few green chillies
a few sultanas

❋

METHOD

1. Grind together the chilli powder, mustard, ginger and garlic. Put the paste into a pan and dissolve in a little vinegar. Add the sugar and salt.

❋

2. Dissolve the cornflour in tepid water and add to the ground ingredients. Heat on a low fire till the mixture becomes somewhat thick. Remove from the fire and cool.

❋

3. Place the fish (fried without batter) on a flat dish. Pour the chilli sauce over the fish.
Fry the red onions whole. Fry the green chillies, slit halfway.
Sprinkle the onions, green chillies and sultanas over the sauce.

❋

This dish goes well with yellow rice.

FAVOURITE DINNERS

Appa (Hopper)

Makes 10 hoppers

INGREDIENTS

1/2 lb rice flour
1/4 t yeast
1 t sugar
1/2 c tepid water

※

12 oz thick coconut milk
1/4 t bicarbonate of soda
1 T coconut milk
※

a hopper pan with lid
gingelly oil

METHOD

1. Sieve the flour. Stir the yeast and sugar in tepid water. Rest it for 15 minutes. Add it to the flour and make a stiff dough with water. Cover and rest it for 30-45 minutes.

※

2. When required, gradually stir in the thick coconut milk, and bicarbonate of soda, dissolved in a little milk.

※

3. Heat a hopper pan. Smear the pan with gingelly oil. Pour a spoonful of batter into the pan and tilt it around to thinly coat a flare around the thick batter in the centre. Cover with a lid. Bake till the edge of the flare begins to brown. Ease the hopper onto a plate.

※

Option : Use instant hopper mixture packet.

Egg Hopper

Egg Hopper

INGREDIENTS

1 egg per hopper

METHOD

1. Make the hopper batter (as given on page 26) After pouring a spoonful into the pan, and tilting it around, break an egg into the centre. Bake as instructed for the plain hopper.

✳

Pittoo

INGREDIENTS

METHOD

1/2 lb rice flour
1/2 lb scraped coconut
salt to taste

1. Mix the flour, coconut and salt in circular movement with your fingers till it forms little grains like peppercorns or sago. A little cold water can be used to get the correct consistency.

a pittoo bamboo with lid
water pot
wooden stick or coconut shell spoon

2. Fill the bamboo with the mixture (fancy moulds can be used). Steam the bamboo on a pot of boiling water. No steam should escape from between the water pot and the bamboo.

   Once the steam starts escaping from the uncovered bamboo top, cover it with a lid. Steam for about 20 minutes till the pittoo is done. Then push out the pittoo onto a dish with a stick. Traditionally the handle of a coconut shell spoon was used.

   While still hot, cut it into 2" long slices. Traditionally, a coconut strand from the nut was used as a knife!

fresh coconut milk
salt

3. Serve with fresh thick coconut milk, to which a dash of salt has been added or with chilli sambol. (see recipe on page 70).

   Any fish, chicken or prawn curry will go well with the pittoo.

Kurakkan Pittoo

INGREDIENTS

1/4 lb rice flour
1/4 lb kurakkan flour
1/2 lb coconut, scraped
salt to taste

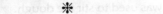

METHOD

1. Mix both the varieties of flour. Proceed as for the rice flour pittoo.

This is extremely nourishing

String Hopper

INGREDIENTS

8 oz rice flour
boiling water
salt to taste

※

a string hopper mould,
cane mats, and oiled
steamer with a lid

※

METHOD

1. Roast the flour well and sieve it into a bowl. Add salt. Use a spoon to make a soft dough with water. Traditionally, the handle of a coconut shell kitchen spoon was used to stir the dough.

※

2. Fill a string hopper mould and press the dough on the oiled mats. Place as many mats as the steamer will hold. Cover and place over the boiling water. Beads of water pouring down the sides of the lid is an indication that the strings are done. Take off the fire and remove the strings from the mats onto a dish.
Repeat the process until all the dough is used up. Cover with a wet muslin cloth to keep the strings moist if they are not going to be used immediately.
Strings freeze well. Steam again for use.

※

(The rice flour, moulds, cane mats and steamers, are all available in the market)

String Hopper Pillau

INGREDIENTS

6-8 oz vegetables (carrots, cabbage, leeks)

❋

4 t oil/ ghee/ margarine
2 oz cadjunuts
2 oz sultanas

❋

2" rampa
a sprig of curry leaves
2" lemon-grass
the cut vegetables

❋

8 oz cooked chicken / prawn, cut into
   bite-size pieces
20 string hoppers
2 cardamoms, crushed
1/2 vegetable stock cube
1/2 c carrot water or plain water
salt and pepper to taste

❋

2 oz cadjunuts, coarsely chopped
2 oz sultanas
2 hard-boiled eggs, quartered

❋

METHOD

1. Cut the vegetables into the size of matchsticks. Parboil carrots. Use the leftover water to dissolve the stock cube.

❋

2. In 1 T oil, fry nuts —do not let them burn. Remove. Fry sultanas. Remove and keep aside.

❋

3. In rest of the oil, fry the herbs, leaves and vegetables.

❋

4. Add the chicken or prawn and fry for three minutes. Add the string hoppers, torn into shreds. Add the cardamoms and stock cube, dissolved in carrot water. Stir lightly, without breaking the strings. Check the salt and pepper.

❋

5. Use the nuts, sultanas and eggs to garnish. The nuts and sultanas can be stirred into the pillau if desired.

❋

CURRIES

Dal Curry

Serves 8

INGREDIENTS

4 oz dal
a few red onions, sliced
1 green chilli, sliced
1 1/2" rampa
1 1/2" lemon-grass
a sprig of curry leaves
1/4 t saffron
1 c second extract of coconut milk
1/4 t salt

✳

1/2 c coconut milk (thick)
1/4 t salt.

✳

1 T oil
a few sliced onions
a few curry leaves
1"–2" rampa
3 dry chillies, quartered
2 cloves of garlic
1/2 t mustard seeds

✳

METHOD

1. Wash the dal. Put in a saucepan with all the listed ingredients and boil till done. Stir occasionally.

✳

2. Add the thick coconut milk and the salt.

✳

3. In another small frying pan, heat oil. Fry the onions, leaves, dry chillies, garlic, till the onions are golden brown in colour. Then add the mustard seeds, till it crackles.
   Add this to the dal curry and keep on the fire for a few minutes.

✳

This is a must in every home. Mysore dal was the favourite but now other varieties have been introduced.

Murunga (Drumsticks)

INGREDIENTS

1 1b murunga
2" rampa
a sprig of curry leaves
1/4 t fenugreek
1" piece cinnamon
2-3 green chillies
1 t saffron
1/2 t salt (less or more)
second extract of 1/2 a coconut

❉

first extract of 1/2 a coconut

❉

METHOD

1. Scrape the fibres off the skin. Cut into finger-length pieces. Add all the ingredients with the coconut milk or water to the murunga; the liquid used must cover the murunga sticks.
Boil till the murunga is cooked.

❉

2. Add the coconut milk. Bring to a boil. Simmer for five minutes.

❉

Murunga has large amounts of protein, calcium and iron and vitamins A and C

Vattakka Curry (Yellow Pumpkin)

INGREDIENTS

1/2 lb pumpkin
1 small Bombay onion
1-2 green chillies

❊

2 T scraped coconut
1/2 t mustard seeds
2 cloves of garlic

❊

1 t Maldive fish (opt.)
a pinch of saffron
a sprig of curry leaves
1/2 t salt
4 oz second extract of coconut milk / water

❊

2 oz first extract of coconut milk

❊

METHOD

1. Leave the skin on and cut the pumpkin into large cubes. Remove the seeds. Chop the onion and chillies.

❊

2. Grind the coconut, mustard and garlic.

❊

3. Except for the coconut mix, add all the ingredients to the second extract, or water, and cook till done.

❊

4. Add the first extract of coconut milk and the coconut mix for thickening. Bring to a boil. Simmer for 10 minutes.

❊

Red pumpkin has vitamin A. It is good for flatulence, constipation and eczema.

Ash Plantain White Curry

Serves 4

INGREDIENTS

2 oz first extract
8 oz second extract

✳

1/2 lb ash plantains
1/2 pint second extract of coconut milk.
1 t fenugreek
1 clove of garlic
1/2" piece ginger, chopped
1" piece cinnamon
1 green chilli
1/2 (Bombay onion), chopped
1 t Maldive fish
1/2 t cumin seeds
1" rampa
a sprig of curry leaves
1/2 t salt
1/2 t saffron

✳

2 oz thick coconut milk

✳

METHOD

1. Squeeze the first and the second extract of coconut milk as needed and keep aside.

✳

2. Peel the plantains and cut 1/4" slices on the slant. Put in a saucepan with all the ingredients. Bring to a boil. Simmer till done.

✳

3. Add the first extract of coconut milk. Bring to a boil and simmer for 10 minutes.

✳

This is great for kids and adults love it too.

Ash Plantain Fried Curry

Serves 4

INGREDIENTS

4 green plantains

※

salt (1/2 lb plantains =1/2 t salt)
a pinch of saffron
oil for frying

※

1 T sliced onion
1 t roasted curry powder
a few curry leaves
1" rampa
1" piece cinnamon
1-2 green chillies, chopped
2 1/2 c coconut milk (1/2 a coconut)

※

METHOD

1. Cut the bananas into small pieces. Do not wash them as you will need double the oil then.

※

2. Mix the plantain pieces with salt and the saffron. Fry in oil till golden in colour (The oil must just cover the pieces).

※

3. Add the listed ingredients. The liquid must cover the plantains. Simmer till the gravy is absorbed.

Kos (Jakfruit Curry)

Serves 6-8

INGREDIENTS

2 oz first extract
8 oz second extract

❊

1/2 lb jakfruit kernels
1 Bombay onion, chopped
1 green chilli, chopped
1" piece cinnamon
1/2 t saffron
1/4 t fenugreek
1/2 t pepper
1/2 t salt
1/2 t curry powder
1/2 pint second extract of coconut
milk

❊

2 oz first extract of coconut milk

❊

METHOD

1. Squeeze the first and the second extract
   of coconut milk as needed and keep
   aside.

   ❊

2. Cut the kernels into strips and wash. Boil
   them with the rest of the ingredients.
   Simmer till tender.

   ❊

3. Add the first extract of coconut milk and
   boil for five minutes.

   ❊

Kos is the only vegetable-cum-fruit today that escapes chemical fertilisers. It provides energy,
protein, iron and calcium and is excellent for lactating mothers. The leaves help in diabetes,
insomnia and snakebite. The ripe kernels provide two varieties of dessert: vala or varaka.
In the rat race of modern life, there are no women even in villages, to remove the sticky
kernels. They eat bread and rush to work. Modern staff in elite homes, might even refuse the
chore. Markets have stepped in to provide the packed kernels.

Polos Curry (Tender Jakfruit)

Serves 8-10

INGREDIENTS

1 lb tender jakfruit
1 goraka or
1 t tamarind
1 coconut

❋

1 T oil
2" rampa
a sprig of curry leaves
3 Bombay onions
2 green chillies
2" piece cinnamon
1/2 t fenugreek
4 t roasted curry powder
coconut milk

❋

salt to taste

❋

METHOD

1. Peel off the skin and cut into somewhat large chunks. Boil the fruit, covered with water to which the goraka or tamarind has been added.
Meanwhile, extract the milk from the coconut and keep it aside.

❋

2. Heat oil and temper the leaves, onions, chillies and cinnamon for 2 minutes. Add the boiled jackfruit, fenugreek, curry powders and the coconut milk to cover the jackfruit pieces.
Simmer till all the milk has almost evaporated, to make a very thick coating for the fruit.

❋

3. Add salt to taste.

❋

This is an excellent substitute for chicken or meat. It used to be simmered overnight on coals but today an electric or gas cooker would have to suffice. Polos enriches breast milk.

Cadjunut Curry

Serves 6

INGREDIENTS

1/2 lb cadjunuts
a pinch of bicarbonate of soda

❋

1 T oil
1" rampa
a sprig of curry leaves
a few red onions, chopped
1 clove
2" piece cinnamon
1 t curry powder
3 green chillies, chopped
1 cardamom
1/4 t saffron
1 c second extract of coconut milk
   or water

❋

salt to taste
1/2 c coconut milk — first extract

❋

METHOD

1. Soak the nuts overnight, or for three hours, with a pinch of bicarbonate of soda.

❋

2. Heat oil and fry the leaves and onions. Add the nuts with all the ingredients and bring to a boil. The liquid must cover the nuts. Simmer till the nuts are tender, for about 10 minutes

3. When the nuts are cooked, add salt and the first extract of coconut milk. Bring to a boil. Simmer for five minutes.

❋

It is almost impossible now to get boiled cadjunuts and we have to make it with the hard, dried nuts available in packets. It is not quite the same thing.

Fried Brinjal Curry

Serves 6

INGREDIENTS

1/2 lb brinjal
1/2 t salt
1/2 t saffron
oil for deep frying

❊

1 t mustard seeds
4 dry chillies
2 T vinegar

❊

3/4 c coconut milk
1-2 t Maldive fish
1 Bombay onion, chopped
2 cloves of garlic
1" piece ginger, chopped
2" rampa
a sprig of curry leaves
1" piece cinnamon
a pinch of fenugreek

❊

1 t sugar

❊

METHOD

1. Cut lengthwise into 2" pieces. Coat with salt and the saffron. Deep fry in oil till golden in colour.

❊

2. Grind the mustard seeds and dry chillies with the vinegar.

❊

3. Put the ground ingredients in a saucepan with the milk and the rest of the ingredients. Boil till the gravy is thick.

❊

4. Add the fried brinjal. Simmer for 10 minutes. Add sugar.

❊

Karavila Curry (Bitter Gourd)

INGREDIENTS

1/2 lb karavila
a few red onions, sliced
1/4 t saffron
3/4 t curry powder
1 tomato, chopped
salt (to taste)

✳

6 oz coconut milk

✳

METHOD

1. Cut each fruit into four, and again into 1 1/2" lengths. Boil all the ingredients together with enough water to almost cover the pieces. Cook uncovered till tender.

✳

2. Add the coconut milk. Bring to a boil and remove from the fire.

✳

The effect of bitter gourd or karavila is similar to insulin. It reduces blood sugar and purifies the blood. Excellent for diseases of the spleen and liver and for asthma. It detoxifies the toxins present in the modern fertilisers.

Thumba Karavila

Serves 4

INGREDIENTS

1/2 lb thumba karavila
1 t salt
1 piece goraka

❉

1 T oil
1 small Bombay onion, chopped
a sprig of curry leaves
1 t chilli powder
1 t Maldive fish
1/2 t cumin seeds
1" piece cinnamon
1 t fenugreek
1 cardamom
1 t curry powder
4 oz second extract of coconut milk
3-4 oz first extract of coconut milk

❉

METHOD

1. Slit into four but do not separate the wedges. Boil with salt and the goraka for 10 minutes. Now separate the wedges and remove the seeds.

❉

2. Heat oil. Fry the onion and curry leaves till golden brown in colour. Add all the ingredients, plus the boiled fruit. Fry for a few minutes.

❉

This variety grows in the dry zone and is similar in value to the common karavila.

Puhul (Ash Pumpkin with Browned Coconut)

Serves 4

INGREDIENTS

1/2 lb ash pumpkin
1 small onion
1 green chilli
1" rampa
a sprig of curry leaves
1/2–3/4 t salt
1/4 t chilli powder
a pinch of saffron
second extract of coconut milk or
    water

1 T scraped coconut
1/2 T rice
2 T coconut milk

METHOD

1. Peel and cut the pumpkin into cubes or small slices. Chop the onion and green chilli and put into a saucepan with the pumpkin and all the other ingredients. Bring to a boil. Simmer till the pumpkin is tender.

2. Roast the coconut and rice. Grind both. Mix them with the milk and add it to the pumpkin. Bring to a boil and simmer till the gravy is thick.

Thalana Batu

INGREDIENTS

8 oz batu
2 oz first extract of coconut milk
8 oz second extract of coconut milk

❋

1 small Bombay onion
2 green chillies
2 cloves of garlic
a few curry leaves
1t chilli powder
1/2t cumin seeds
1t grated Maldive fish
1 1/2t curry powder
salt to taste
8 oz second extract of coconut milk

❋

2 oz first extract of coconut milk

❋

METHOD

1. Cut the batu in halves or quarters according to the size of the fruit. Scoop out the seeds. Extract the coconut milk as mentioned.

❋

2. Chop the onion, chillies and garlic. Put in a saucepan with the batu and all the listed ingredients. Add the second extract of milk and bring to a boil. Cook till the batu is tender.

❋

3. Add the first extract of coconut milk. Bring to a boil. Simmer for two minutes.

❋

Batu comes in many varieties elabatu, thibbatu, welbatu, vambatu, thalanabatu and katuwelbatu.
Thalanabatu stimulates the heart, purifies the blood, benefits ailments like stones in the bladder, catarrh and asthma. Vedas swear by every part of the thalanabatu tree.

Thibbatu

Serves 4

INGREDIENTS

1/2 lb thibbatu

1 T oil
a sprig of curry leaves
1 small onion, chopped
1 t chilli powder
1/2 t salt
2 oz coconut milk
1 t curry powder
a pinch of saffron

METHOD

1. Wash and boil the fruits with enough water to cover them. Crush them with a spoon to remove the seeds.

2. Heat oil. Fry the curry leaves and onion for two minutes. Add the rest of the ingredients and bring to a boil.
Add the fruits and simmer for 10 minutes.

For asthma, coughs and diseases of the respiratory system.

Innala White Curry

Serves 4

INGREDIENTS

8 oz innala

❋

a few red onions, chopped
1 green chilli, chopped
2" rampa
a sprig of curry leaves
1/4 t saffron
1/2 t salt (or to taste)

❋

1/4 pint coconut milk

❋

METHOD

1. Soak the innala for a few hours and scrape the skin off. Wash well.

❋

2. Add all the ingredients to the innala. Cover with water and boil till tender.

❋

3. Add the coconut milk. Bring to a boil and simmer for five minutes. Check the salt.

❋

Garlic Curry

INGREDIENTS

Serves 6

2 whole pods of garlic
5 red onions
2 green chillies
1/2 t fenugreek
a pinch of saffron
1/4 t chilli powder
2 t roasted curry powder
1/2 t salt
1/2 c second extract of coconut milk

❋

1/2 c first extract of coconut milk.

❋

METHOD

1. Clean the garlic segments off its skin but keep the segments whole. Chop the onions and green chillies. Scrape the coconut and extract milk; the first and the second extracts. Mix all the ingredients with the second extract only. Boil till the garlic is cooked.

2. Add the first extract of coconut milk and boil till the liquid has almost evaporated and thickly coats the garlic cloves.

❋

Garlic slows down the process of ageing, is used in the treatment of indigestion, paralysis and loss of appetite. Garlic in bees' honey is an age-old recipe.

Kohila Burgers

INGREDIENTS

8 oz kohila, mashed
1 1/2 c water
1/4 t saffron
1 goraka or 1/2 T lime juice
salt to taste

❋

1/2 a large onion, chopped
1/2" piece ginger
4 cloves of garlic

❋

1/2 T oil/butter
1 t curry powder
1 t chilli powder
10 cadjunuts, chopped
1/4 T flour
1/4 t cardamom powder
1/4 t nutmeg powder
salt to taste

❋

4 oz tomato, peeled and diced
3/4 c bread crumbs
1 egg

❋

oil for shallow frying
chilli sauce/tomato sauce
fried onion rings
a few sprigs of curry leaves or
murunga leaves

❋

METHOD

1. Clean and cube the kohila, removing threads before cutting. Boil the kohila with the listed ingredients for 15 minutes. Drain the water. Leave to cool.

❋

2. Mash or mince the boiled kohila to a paste in a food processor. Grind the onion, garlic and ginger to a paste.

❋

3. Heat oil/butter. Fry the ground mixture. Remove from the fire. Stir in the listed ingredients. Add salt.

❋

4. Add the mashed kohila, tomato, breadcrumbs and finally the egg. Mix well. Refrigerate for one hour.

❋

5. Remove from the fridge and divide into 4-5 portions. Shape into flat cutlets. Shallow fry on medium heat. Garnish with the fried onion rings and leaves. Serve with chilli sauce or tomato sauce.

❋

Traditional saying: 'If you have a temper, eat kohila'. It is excellent for urinary diseases and cleanses the bowels.

Dal Curry

Capsicum and Potato Curry

Capsicum and Potato Curry

Serves 4

INGREDIENTS

200gms potatoes
12 capsicums

3T oil
2" rampa
3" lemon-grass
12 curry leaves

1 scraped T Maldive fish
1/2 t chilli powder
1/2t sugar
salt to taste
2 big red tomatoes, chopped
1 T water

juice of 1/2 a lime

METHOD

1. Boil the potatoes and cut in quarters. Keep aside.
   De seed the capsicums and cut in large slant slices.

2. Heat oil in a saucepan. Fry the sliced capsicums and herbs.

3. Add the listed ingredients.

4. Stir and cook for a few minutes. Add the potatoes and lime.
   Stir carefully. Cover and cook on a low flame for a few minutes.

Mock Prawns in Ginger Sauce

Serves 5

INGREDIENTS

25 pink jambu fruits
3 c water
1 t salt

*

2 T cornflour
2 eggs
salt to taste
toothpicks
oil for deep frying

*

2 cloves of garlic
2" piece ginger
1 T oil / butter
1 large onion, diced
1 t chilli powder
3 T sugar
1 c ginger beer
1 T tomato sauce
1 T vinegar
salt to taste

*

METHOD

1. Split the jambus into two and remove the seeds. Place in water and add salt. Soak for half an hour. Drain. Pat dry.

*

2. Make the batter with the cornflour, eggs and salt. Thread the jambus on toothpicks. Dip each in the batter and fry till done. Drain well. Serve with the ginger sauce.

*

3. Sauce: Make a paste of the garlic and ginger. Keep aside. Melt butter and fry the onion till soft. Stir in the garlic and ginger paste. Add the chilli powder. Cook a few minutes.
Add the sugar and ginger beer. Simmer for 10 minutes. Add the sauce and vinegar. Check the salt. Garnish with ginger leaves.

Stuffed Capsicum Curry

Serves 6

INGREDIENTS

12 capsicums
75gms scraped Maldive fish
75gms shredded onion
salt to taste
a little lime juice

❋

oil for frying
a thick thread

❋

1 c coconut milk
25gms scraped Maldive fish
25gms scraped onion
2" rampa
stem of lemon-grass.
10 curry leaves
1 tomato, chopped
salt to taste

❋

juice of 1/2 a lime
a pinch of saffron

❋

METHOD

1. Slit the capsicums lengthwise and remove the seeds. Stuff each with a mixture of the listed ingredients.

❋

2. Tie each capsicum with a thread and fry in oil. Remove from the pan and keep aside. Remove the threads.

❋

3. Now prepare the gravy. Assemble in a saucepan the listed ingredients.

❋

4. Boil, stirring till the gravy is thick. Put in the stuffed capsicums. Add the lime and saffron. Cook for a few minutes on a low flame.

❋

Cooked Cucumber

INGREDIENTS

2 medium cucumbers
salt to taste

1 oz mustard seeds
1 oz artificial vinegar
salt to taste
1 c thick coconut milk

METHOD

1. Peel and cut the cucumbers into sections. Remove the seeds and slice thinly. Let it stand in salted water for half an hour. Squeeze out all the water.

2. Grind the mustard seeds to a paste with a little vinegar. Add this, with the remaining vinegar and salt, to the coconut milk. Put on the fire. When the milk is boiling, add the cucumber. Cook for a few minutes. Add more milk if it is too dry. Do not overboil the cucumber.

Chilli Fish

Serves 8

INGREDIENTS

1 lb fish, white or red,
salt to taste
2 green chillies, split into two
1" rampa
a sprig of curry leaves
3-4 t chilli powder
3 cloves of garlic
1" piece ginger, chopped
1 T tamarind juice
2" piece cinnamon
2 oz water
1/4 t pepper powder

METHOD

1. Cut the fish in eight pieces. Mix all the ingredients. Bring to a boil and simmer till the gravy is thick.

Fish Ambul Thiyal (with goraka)

INGREDIENTS

Serves 4

METHOD

8 oz blood fish (Bala or Kelavallo)
4 pieces goraka
4 cloves
1/2" piece ginger, chopped
1 T chilli powder
2 cloves of garlic
a sprig of curry leaves
salt to taste
4 oz water, if fish is in one layer and
more water for a double layer

✳

1. Cut thick pieces and wash the fish well. Soak the goraka for half an hour. Put the fish and all the ingredients into a saucepan (preferably a clay chatty) and mix well.
   Simmer till the fish is cooked and the gravy has almost evaporated.

✳

Fish in White Gravy

INGREDIENTS

1 lb white fish
1 t salt
2 green chillies
a pinch of saffron
2 oz onion, chopped
2" rampa
1" lemon-grass
a sprig of curry leaves
2 cloves of garlic, chopped
1" piece ginger, chopped
1/4 t fenugreek
1/4 pint second extract of coconut
  milk

1/2 pint first extract of coconut milk.
1/2t mustard seeds
a little vinegar
juice of 1/2 a lime.

✷

METHOD

1. Wash the fish well. Cut into eight pieces. Put all the ingredients in a saucepan. Boil till the fish is cooked for 10-15 minutes.

2. Ground the mustard seeds. Add the first extract of coconut milk and the ground mustard with a little vinegar, and lime. Shake the pan to mix well. Keep for a few minutes on the fire and then remove.

✷

Fish Tamarind Curry

INGREDIENTS

1 lb fish
1 T tamarind in 1/2 c water
1/2 c hot water
1 1/2 T curry powder
1 t salt
1/4 t saffron
1 t chilli powder

3 T oil
a sprig of curry leaves
1/4 t fenugreek
1 onion, chopped
2 cloves of garlic

METHOD

1. Marinate the fish with all the ingredients.

2. Heat oil. Fry the leaves and fenugreek for one minute. Add the onion and garlic. Saute till the onion is golden in colour. Add the fish and marinade. Cover. Simmer for 10 minutes. Uncover and simmer for 10 more minutes.

Fried Fish Curry

INGREDIENTS

2 cloves of garlic
1" piece ginger
vinegar

1/4 lb slice of fish
juice of half a lime
1/4 t pepper
1/2 t salt
1/4 t saffron

oil
1/4 t fenugreek
1/4 t chilli powder
2 green chillies
milk of half a coconut
1" rampa and lemon-grass
a sprig of curry leaves
1/4 lb onions, sliced

METHOD

1. Grind the garlic and ginger with a little vinegar.

2. Wash the slice of fish. Do not cut it. Marinate it in lime, pepper, salt, saffron and the ground mixture for one hour.

3. Fry the slice of fish till it is golden in colour. Add the marinade and all the ingredients. Bring to a boil. Simmer till the gravy is like a thick sauce.

Fish Smore

INGREDIENTS

1 lb fish, cut into two slices
1 t salt
1/2 t pepper (or more)
1/2 t saffron
1 T ghee

✳

8 oz boiled potatoes, quartered.
8 oz boiled carrot, chinese cut
1 Bombay onion, quartered
a few capsicums, chinese cut
1" piece ginger
2 cloves of garlic
1" rampa
a few curry leaves and lemon-grass
1 t chilli powder
2 t curry powder
1 T tamarind
1" piece cinnamon
1/4 c coconut milk

✳

1 c or less of coconut milk
1 T flour

✳

METHOD

1. Rub the salt, pepper and saffron on the slices of fish. Fry in ghee till golden in colour. Remove.

✳

2. Add all the vegetables, spices, leaves and the coconut milk. Simmer till the fish and vegetables are done. Remove the fish onto a dish and saute the vegetables.

✳

3. Add the coconut milk. Thicken with the flour if necessary. Pour over the fish.

✳

Seer Dried Fish Moju

Serves 8

INGREDIENTS

4 oz dried fish, seer is best.
4 oz dried prawns
2 T oil

✳

8 oz red onions, whole
4 oz capsicums, cut into 2" pieces

✳

4 oz vinegar
1 oz dry chillies
1 oz mustard seeds

✳

2 oz sugar
salt to taste

METHOD

1. Cut the fish in cubes. Wash and dry the prawns, if necessary. Fry both of them separately in oil. Keep aside.

✳

2. Fry the onions and capsicums for a minute on a low flame to avoid burning. Keep aside.

✳

3. Fry the dry chillies and grind them with a little vinegar.
   Grind the mustard with a little vinegar and then fry it.

✳

4. Mix all the ingredients in a saucepan. Add the sugar, rest of the unused vinegar, and salt if necessary. Bring to a boil. If it is too thick, add half a cup of water and simmer for five minutes.

✳

Prawn Curry

INGREDIENTS

1/2 lb fresh prawns
1 c extract of coconut milk

✳

1 T chopped red onion
2 cloves of garlic, chopped
a piece of ginger, chopped
2 green chillies, cut
1/2 c second extract of coconut milk
1" rampa
a sprig of curry leaves
1 t chilli powder
1 " piece cinnamon
a pinch of saffron
1 small tomato
salt to taste

✳

1 T grated coconut
1/2 t uncooked rice
1/2 c first extract of coconut milk
2 t lime juice

✳

1/2 T ghee
a sprig of curry leaves.

✳

a handful of drumstick leaves
(Murunga Kola)

METHOD

1. Remove the prawn heads and the shells. Devein. Wash well. Extract the coconut milk — the first and the second extracts. Keep aside.

✳

2. Put the prawns in a saucepan with all the ingredients in the first and the second list. Cook till the prawns are nearly done. Add salt.

✳

3. Grind the coconut and rice together. Add it to the prawns with the first extract of coconut milk. Add the lime juice and cook till the prawns are done.

✳

4. Heat ghee and saute the curry leaves. Add the prawn mix and simmer for 10-15 minutes.

✳

5. Sprinkle the drumstick leaves. They are both decorative and medicinal, and prevent allergic reactions to prawns.

Dry Prawn Curry

Serves 4

INGREDIENTS

1/2 lb prawns, fresh

❋

3 T oil
a sprig of curry leaves
2" rampa
1 Bombay onion
2 cloves of garlic

❋

a pinch of saffron
1/2 t salt
1" piece cinnamon
1 cardamom
1 clove
2 t chilli powder (preferably coarse)

❋

1/2 t lime juice.

❋

METHOD

1. Remove the heads of the prawns. Devein and wash well.

❋

2. Heat oil. Fry the leaves, chopped onion and garlic till golden in colour.

❋

3. Add the rest of the ingredients. Cook till the prawns are done.
(This can be kept for a few days.)

❋

4. Add the lime juice.

❋

Dried Sprats Fry

INGREDIENTS

2 oz dried sprats
1 piece goraka

✳

2 T oil
1 Bombay onion, chopped
a handful of curry leaves
1 clove of garlic, chopped
salt to taste
chilli powder (1 t or more to taste)

✳

METHOD

1. Remove the heads and wash them well with the goraka.

✳

2. Heat oil. Mix all the ingredients together and fry for five minutes. Simmer for 10 minutes. Add the chilli and salt to taste.

✳

Dried Sprats Curry

INGREDIENTS

8 oz dried sprats
half a coconut

1 onion, chopped
2" rampa
a sprig of curry leaves
1 tomato, chopped
1 goraka
2 green chillies, chopped
a pinch of saffron
salt to taste
2 t chilli powder
second extract of coconut milk

first extract of coconut milk

METHOD

1. Remove the heads of the sprats. Wash well and drain. Extract the milk from half a coconut — the first and the second extracts. Keep aside.

2. Add all the ingredients to the washed sprats. Bring to a boil in water, or the second extract of coconut milk.

3. Add the first extract. Bring to a boil and simmer for five minutes.

Chicken Curry

INGREDIENTS

2 3/4 lbs chicken
2 t salt
4-6 t chilli powder
2 t curry powder, roasted
2 t curry powder, plain
1/2 t saffron

❋

1 T oil
1 Bombay onion, chopped
1" rampa
a few curry leaves
3 green chillies
1/4 t fennel seeds
2 cloves of garlic, chopped
1" piece ginger, chopped
1/4 t cinnamon powder
1/8 c vinegar
3 T tamarind, after squeezing it in
water

❋

2 c thick coconut milk

❋

METHOD

1. Cleaned chicken pieces are available in the market these days. Rub the pieces with the salt, chilli powder, curry powders and saffron.

❋

2. Put one tablespoon of oil in a saucepan. Add the chicken with all the ingredients Close the lid and simmer for 45 minutes. Stir occasionally.

❋

3. Remove the chicken. Add the milk to the remnants in the saucepan and simmer for 10 minutes. Take off the fire.
   If more gravy is desired, increase the quantity of the coconut milk.

❋

Soya Curry

INGREDIENTS

4 oz dried soya cubes
2 cloves of garlic
2 t ginger

2 t chilli powder
2 t curry powder

❋

2 T oil/margarine
1 Bombay onion, sliced
2-3 green chillies, sliced
1" rampa
a sprig of curry leaves

❋

1 c coconut milk
1 t tamarind
1/4 t salt

❋

METHOD

1. Pour boiling water on the cubes to cover them. Soak them for 10 minutes. Drain and squeeze out all the water.
   Grind the garlic and ginger. Keep aside.

2. Add the chilli and curry powders to the drained soya.

❋

3. Heat oil till it is very hot. Fry the onion. When translucent, add the ginger-garlic paste. Add the green chillies and curry leaves. Add the soya. Cook for three minutes.

❋

4. Make a paste with tamarind and a little water. Add the coconut milk, tamarind and salt. When boiling, remove from the fire. If the gravy is too watery, boil and reduce to a thick sauce consistency.

❋

Fried Egg Curry

INGREDIENTS

4 eggs
3 T oil

❋

1 T ghee / margarine
1 T onion
2 green chillies
1" rampa
2 1/2" lemon-grass
1/2 a sprig of curry leaves
1 t chilli powder
milk of half a coconut
2" piece cinnamon
1 t curry powder
1 t Maldive fish

❋

the fried eggs
salt to taste
a squirt of lime juice

❋

METHOD

1. Hard boil the eggs. Shell them and fry in oil till they are golden in colour.

❋

2. To make the gravy, fry the onions, leaves and green chillies. Add the rest of the ingredients.

❋

3. When it comes to a boil, add the eggs and salt. Remove from the fire and add the lime juice.

❋

MELLUNS, SAMBOLA AND PICKLES

Ash Plantain Mellun (skins only)

Serves 4

INGREDIENTS

8 oz plantain skins
salt to taste
1 t lime
water

1 small Bombay onion
1 green chilli
a sprig of curry leaves
a pinch of saffron
2 oz scraped coconut

METHOD

1. Shred the skins finely. Boil them with salt and the lime in a little water till tender and all water has evaporated.

2. Chop the onion and green chilli. Add with all the rest of the ingredients to the boiled skins. Toss over the fire till the coconut is cooked. Do not overcook.

Coconut Mellun

INGREDIENTS

1 Bombay onion, chopped fine
1 green chilli, chopped
a pinch of saffron
a sprig of curry leaves
1 goraka
2 oz water

✻

1/2 a coconut, scraped
salt to taste
juice of 1 lime

✻

METHOD

1. Cook all the ingredients till the onion is soft.

✻

2. Add the coconut. Cook for a few minutes. Add the lime juice and salt to taste.

✻

Kathuru Murunga Mellun

Serves 4

INGREDIENTS

1/4 lb kathuru murunga
1 oz water
1 medium onion
1 green chilli

8 oz scraped coconut
salt to taste

✳

METHOD

1. Finely shred the leaves and sprinkle some water on them. Add the onion and chilli. Toss on fire for about four minutes, to take the rawness out.

    ✳

2. Add the coconut and salt. Stir over fire to mix well for one minute.

    ✳

These leaves do not need washing in condys crystals or any other disinfectant as they grow on trees.

Lunu Miris (Chilli Sambol)

INGREDIENTS

2 oz dried chillies (red)
2 oz red onions
1/2 oz Maldive fish
lime juice
salt to taste

METHOD

1. Grind all the ingredients together. (Traditionally it was done on a slab of granite with a rolling pin, also of granite). Add salt and the lime to taste.

❋

Seeni Sambol

INGREDIENTS

1 lb red onions, finely chopped
3/4 c oil

❊

2" rampa
a sprig of curry leaves
2" lemon-grass
3 cardamoms
3 cloves
2" piece cinnamon
1" piece ginger
6 cloves of garlic

❊

2 T chilli powder
2 1/2 oz or 4 oz Maldive fish

❊

2 oz tamarind
1/4 c coconut milk or water

❊

1 t salt
2 t sugar
1/2 a lime

❊

METHOD

1. Fry the onions in hot oil till golden brown in colour. Stir constantly.

❊

2. Take 2T of oil and fry the herbs and spices on a very low flame.

❊

3. Add the chilli powder and Maldive fish according to taste.

❊

4. Add the browned onions and tamarind soaked in coconut milk or water.

❊

5. Add the salt, sugar and lime juice.

❊

The onion is an aphrodisiac and is considered as an elixir of life. It checks hypertension and stabilises blood pressure.

Gotukola Sambol

Serves 4

INGREDIENTS

4 oz gotukola
1 small Bombay onion
1 small tomato
1-2 green chillies
1 t Maldive fish
3 oz coconut, scraped
1/4 t salt
juice of 1/2 a lime

✱

METHOD

1. Weigh leaves after picking the fresh leaves and tender stems for use. Shred fine, hand cut is best. Chop the onion, tomato and green chillies. Grate Maldive fish. Mix everything.

✱

Gotukola has loads of vitamin A.

Coconut Sambol

INGREDIENTS

4 oz scraped coconut
1 medium Bombay onion
1-2 green chillies (depends on how
    hot you like it)
1 clove of garlic
1 1/2 T chilli powder
salt to taste
1/4 t pepper powder
juice of 1/2 a lime

❋

METHOD

1. Mix all the ingredients in a food
   processor or mixer. It is ready for eating.

❋

Easy Blachan Sambol

INGREDIENTS

2 oz dried prawns

❋

1-2 cloves of garlic
2 slices of ginger

❋

1/2 - 1 T chilli powder
salt to taste
lime juice to taste

❋

METHOD

1. Wash the dried prawns. Then roast and pound them finely. (Use a grinder or a food processor)

   ❋

2. Grind the garlic and ginger. Add them to the pounded prawns.

   ❋

3. Add the chilli powder, salt and lime juice to taste.

   ❋

Kehel Muwa Fry (Plantain Flower)

INGREDIENTS

1 1/2 lb kehel muwa
8 oz onions
2 oz dried sprats

3-4 oz tamarind
2" rampa
a sprig of curry leaves
2" lemon-grass
4 cloves of garlic, chopped
1/2-1" piece ginger, sliced
salt to taste
1 1/2 t sugar

METHOD

1. Chop the muwa and onions finely. Separately deep fry them and the sprats till crisp.

2. Soak the tamarind in very little water and squeeze the juice.
   Saute the leaves, garlic and ginger. Toss in the fried ingredients and add the tamarind juice, salt and sugar.

Bitter Gourd Sambol (Karavila)

INGREDIENTS

4 oz bitter gourds
2 oz red onions
1 green chilli
1 small tomato

❋

1/4 t salt
1/4 t saffron
oil for frying

❋

1 t Maldive fish
1 t lime juice
salt to taste

❋

METHOD

1. Slice the gourds into thin rounds. Slice the onions, green chilli and tomato.

❋

2. Mix the gourd slices with salt and the saffron. Heat oil to cover the base of a pan and fry the slices till golden brown and crisp.

❋

3. Mix the fried gourd with the onions, green chillies, tomato, Maldive fish and lime juice. Add salt according to taste.

❋

Lime Pickle

INGREDIENTS

6 limes
1 oz vinegar
4 oz sugar
1 oz salt

METHOD

1. Prick the limes with a fork.
   Bring the vinegar, sugar and salt to a boil.
   Add the limes. When yellow in colour, remove and cool.
   Put into airtight bottles and leave for two weeks.

Malay Pickle

INGREDIENTS

1/2 oz dried chillies
1/2" slice of ginger
2 cloves of garlic
1/4 oz mustard seeds
vinegar

3 oz red onions
1/2 a pickled lime, chopped
2 oz capsicums, cut into 1" pieces
1/2 oz dried billing, chopped
1 oz dried mango, chopped
1/2 oz sugar
2 oz dates, chopped
salt

METHOD

1. No cooking. Only grinding!
   Grind the chillies, ginger, garlic and mustard with a little vinegar and make a thick paste of dropping consistency.

2. Add the paste to the rest of the ingredients. Check to see if you need more of salt and sugar. Cool and bottle.

Brinjal Moju

Serves 15 or more

INGREDIENTS

1/2 lb brinjal, cut into pieces
4 oz capsicums, cut into 1" pieces
4 oz red onions
2 oz dates, stoned and halved
carrots or dried sprats, cut into pieces

❋

3 oz vinegar
1/2 T mustard seeds
1/2 oz ginger
5 cloves of garlic

❋

2 1/4 oz sugar
1/2 t salt
1 T chilli powder
1/4 t pepper

❋

METHOD

1. Fry separately and drain all the vegetables.

❋

2. Grind the mustard, ginger and garlic with some of the vinegar.

❋

3. Boil the ground mixture with the sugar, salt, chilli powder and whatever remains of the vinegar. Cool a little. Add the fried vegetables and simmer for two minutes.

❋

Bottle and freeze if you like.

Bibikkan

INGREDIENTS

1/2 a coconut
1 lb jaggery
8 oz sugar
salt to taste

2 oz wheat flour
4 oz cadjunuts
4 oz sultanas
1 oz ginger preserve
1/4 t cloves
1/4 t cardamoms
1/2 t cinnamon
1 t grated rind of lime

✳

METHOD

1. Scrape the coconut and extract the milk from it without adding any water. Add the milk to the jaggery and sugar and bring it to a boil. Add salt.
   Add the scraped coconut to the mixture and cook till it is sticky. Remove from the fire.

3. Add the flour and mix well. Add the rest of the ingredients. Mix well.
   Bake at 325°F till the skewer comes out clean.

✳

Kavun

INGREDIENTS

8 oz rice flour
8 oz coconut treacle,
(coconut treacle is a variety of treacle)

❋

a deep hopper-like pan
oil for frying
an ekel
a kitchen spoon

❋

METHOD

1. Mix the flour and coconut treacle. The correct consistency of the batter will come only with experience.

❋

2. Let the batter stand for half an hour. Heat the oil for deep frying. Pour half a spoon of batter into the oil. As it begins to fry, the centre will rise.
Pour a little more batter into the centre and insert an ekel in the middle of the cake. Do not pierce it through. Keep twisting the ekel round and round and at the same time splashing the boiling oil on the cake with a spoon. This will produce a knot at the top, which is essential.
Get the correct shape by pressing down with a spoon. It must have a nice brown colour when done.
The oil must not be too hot or the cakes will remain raw inside.

❋

There can be no Sinhala New Year (in April) without kavun. The westernised cake-making elite run in circles to procure them. The bakers now fulfil this need.

Kokis with Rice Flour (Koekjes in Dutch)

INGREDIENTS

Makes about 18 kokis

1 kokis mould
1/2 lb rice flour
milk of 1/2 a coconut
1/4 egg
1/2 t salt
saffron

❋

oil for frying

METHOD

1. A kokis mould is necessary.
   Mix the flour with the coconut milk. Add the beaten egg, salt and saffron. Let the batter rest for an hour.

   ❋

2. Heat oil. Dip the mould in the oil and then in the batter and then back in the oil, to fry it crisply.

   ❋

Kokis with Wheat Flour

Makes about 18-20 kokis

INGREDIENTS

1/4 lb wheat flour
1 egg
8-12 oz cow's milk
1/2 t salt

❋

oil for frying
a kokis mould

❋

METHOD

1. Beat the egg with 8 oz milk.
   Add to the flour to form a thin batter.
   Add more milk if necessary. Add salt to taste.

❋

2. Fry as in the rice flour recipe (page 82)

❋

Puhuldosi (White Pumpkin Preserve)

8 pieces

INGREDIENTS

1/2 lb pumpkin

✻

1 lb sugar
2 oz semolina
1/4 t cardamom powder

✻

1/2 t rose essence and colouring

✻

METHOD

1. Weigh the pumpkin only after grating it and squeezing out the water with a muslin cloth.

✻

2. Stir the pumpkin and sugar on a moderate fire for about 15 minutes. Lower the flame. Add the semolina and cardamom powder and continue stirring till the sugar begins to crystallise on the sides of the pan.

✻

3. Add the rose essence and colouring (pale green, pink, yellow) just before taking it off the fire. Transfer onto a flat dish and cut into squares before it cools.

✻

Puhuldosi experts make roses out of this preserve.

Thala Guli (Gingelly Balls)

About 20

INGREDIENTS

1/2 lb gingelly seeds

✻

1/2 lb jaggery
salt to taste

✻

METHOD

1. Wash, strain and dry the tiny seeds. Pound them.

    ✻

2. Add the jaggery and salt. Continue pounding till an oily paste is formed. Shape into lime-sized balls.

    ✻

Wandu Hopper (a teatime snack)

INGREDIENTS

1 lb rice flour
4 oz coconut water

✳

8 oz coconut milk
5 oz jaggery
a pinch of bicarbonate of soda
a pinch of salt

✳

a muslin cloth
a kenda leaf (or a banana leaf).
scraped coconut

✳

METHOD

1. Put the flour in a bowl and mix it with the coconut water. Knead well. Cover and keep for four hours.

✳

2. Add the coconut milk gradually. Add the jaggery, salt and bicarbonate of soda. Mix well. Cover with a muslin cloth and let it rise for about three hours.

✳

3. Boil a saucepan of water — it should be half full. Tie the muslin cloth loosely on the mouth of the pan.
   Place a kenda leaf in the middle of the cloth and put a spoonful of batter on it. Cover and steam till it is cooked. It should be well risen and split in the middle. Serve with scraped coconut.

✳

Lavariya

INGREDIENTS

8 oz riceflour
8 oz coconut treacle

8 oz rice flour
boiling water
salt to taste

✳

kenda leaves or banana leaves
coconut treacle mixture

✳

steamer
string hopper mats

✳

METHOD

1. Make the coconut treacle mixture (as on page 81). Keep aside.

    ✳

2. Roast the flour well and sieve into a bowl. Add salt. Add enough boiling water to make a stiff dough as for string hoppers.

    ✳

3. Put the batter into a string hopper mould and squeeze onto a leaf like for string hoppers. Put a tablespoon of the coconut treacle mixture in the centre and fold the leaf into two.

    ✳

4. Slip the folded lavariyas out of the leaves onto the oiled string hopper mats and steam them till done.

    ✳

Aggala

INGREDIENTS

1/4 lb parboiled rice
1/2 lb coconut treacle
a pinch of salt.

❋

1/4 t pepper

METHOD

1. Roast and pound the rice. Sieve it. Put the treacle in a pan with salt. Boil till it is thick. Remove from the fire.

❋

2. Reserve a quarter of the sieved rice for coating the aggala later. Mix the pepper with the rest of the rice and add it to the treacle. Mix till it forms a stiff paste. Before it cools, make it into lime sized balls. Coat well with the reserved powdered rice.

❋

Cadjunut Aluwa (with milk)

12 pieces

INGREDIENTS

50 cadjunuts
1/2 lb sugar
1/2 oz butter
3 oz milk

✳

1/2-1 t rose essence

✳

METHOD

1. Chop the nuts fine. Put the sugar, butter and milk into a saucepan and stir it over a fire till the sugar melts.

✳

2. Add the nuts and cook them till the mixture thickens. Remove from the fire. Add the essence. Put into a dish rinsed with water. Cut when it is nearly cold.

✳

Jaggery and Coconut (Pani-pol)

INGREDIENTS

4 oz jaggery
4 oz scraped coconut

❋

1/2" piece cinnamon
a pinch of salt
1/4 t rice flour

❋

METHOD

1. Scrape the jaggery and coconut. Put the jaggery and 1 1/2 T water in a pan and heat on a low flame. Stir the mixture till it thickens, over low heat.

❋

2. Add the coconut, cinnamon and salt. When the mixture is thick, add the rice flour and stir for a few minutes longer.

❋

If you like the flavour of sweet cumin seeds, add a pinch of roasted sweet cumin seeds to the rice flour.

Cadjunut and Jaggery Aluwa

About 12 pieces

INGREDIENTS

4 oz cadjunuts
4 oz sugar
4 oz jaggery

❋

1 oz butter

METHOD

1. Cut the nuts fine. Boil sugar and jaggery with one-fourth of a tumbler of water, till thick.

❋

2. Add the nuts and butter. Cook till it leaves the sides of the pan. Transfer to a greased dish and cut into squares.

❋

Ijzer Koekjes

INGREDIENTS

4 oz wheat flour
4 oz sugar
1 egg yolk
1/2 egg white
1/2 cup coconut milk
1/2 t powdered cinnamon
a pinch of powdered clove
salt to taste

❉

an ijzer mould
oil or butter

❉

round sticks, 1/2" in diameter

❉

METHOD

1. Mix the flour and sugar together. Add the beaten egg. Gradually add the coconut milk, powdered cinnamon, clove and salt. Mix well.

❉

2. Heat the ijzer mould and smear it with oil or butter. Pour a tablespoon of batter into it. Close the ijzer mould and place it over a hot fire. When the koekje is browned on one side, turn it and brown it on the other side.

❉

3. Be ready with a round stick. As soon as each koekje is taken off the ijzer mould, roll it around the stick and slip it off into an airtight tin.

❉

Breudher

INGREDIENTS

1 lb bread dough

✳

1/2 lb sugar
12 egg yolks
1/2 lb butter

✳

1/2 lb sultanas
a little flour

✳

METHOD

1. Buy bread dough from the baker, put it on a pastry board and knead well till firm.

✳

2. Add the sugar, yolks and butter in small quantities. The mixture must be firm and not watery.

✳

3. Toss the sultanas in some flour and add it to the dough. Knead well for 45 minutes. Pour into the greased pans and keep in the hot sun for an hour. Bake at 350°F till light brown in colour.

✳

This is a Dutch legacy which appears on the tables at Christmas and now even for the Sinhala-Tamil New Year. It is eaten with butter and cheese.

Love Cake

INGREDIENTS

75 cadjunuts
1/4 lb semolina
6 eggs
1/2 lb sugar

❋

1/4 lb butter
1 1/2 oz rose water
11/2 oz brandy
1/2 t cinnamon powder
1/2 t cardamom powder
1/2 t nutmeg powder

❋

3 egg whites
a flat tin
greaseproof paper

❋

METHOD

1. Finely grind the cadjunuts. Slightly roast the semolina. Separate the three egg whites from the six eggs and keep aside. Beat the yolks of all the eggs with the sugar. Beat well till bubbles appear.

❋

2. Add the butter, semolina, nuts, flavours and spices.

❋

3. Whisk the egg whites and stir them into the batter. Pour onto a flat tin, lined with greaseproof paper. Bake at 350°F. It should be nicely browned.

❋

Jaggery Cake

INGREDIENTS

1/4 lb jaggery
1/4 lb cadjunuts

1/2 lb semolina
1/4 lb butter

✳

3 eggs
1/2 lb sugar

✳

1 t spices (cloves, nutmeg, cardamoms)
1 1/2 T rose essence
2 t vanilla essence

✳

1/4 c coconut milk
cake tin 6" x 6"

✳

METHOD

1. Finely scrape the jaggery. Pound half the cadjunuts and chop the other halves.

✳

2. Slightly roast the semolina and mix it with butter.

3. Separate the whites from the yolks. Beat the yolks with the sugar and scraped jaggery for 1/2 an hour.

✳

4. Fold the butter and semolina into the beaten yolk mixture. Add the chopped cadjunuts, spices, essences and the well beaten egg whites.

✳

5. Add the coconut milk. Bake at 200° F for about an hour. Cover with a piece of foil if the top is getting burnt.

✳

Kalu Dodol

INGREDIENTS

1 1/4 lb jaggery
2 oz cadjunuts
3 pint coconut milk
4 oz rice flour
a brass spoon

✳

1/4 t cardamom powder
2 oz slivered nuts

✳

a flat pan

✳

METHOD

1. Scrape the jaggery. Sliver the nuts. In a very heavy bottom saucepan, gradually add the milk to the flour. Add the jaggery. Keep on the fire and stir all the time with a brass spoon. There should not be any lumps.

✳

2. As it thickens, oil appears on the surface which must be removed with a spoon. Stirring must be non-stop. Stir till it becomes thick and dark. Three-quarter of the way, add the cardamoms and slivered nuts. When the mixture comes off the sides of the pan in one mass, remove it from the fire.

✳

3. Pour onto a flat pan and cut into pieces when cold.

✳

Sago Dodol

Serves 6

INGREDIENTS

12 oz riceflour
1/2 t salt

a muslin cloth
a steamer with a lid

✳

4 oz jaggery, scraped
1/2" piece of cinnamon
3 oz coconut milk
a pinch of sweet cumin seeds

✳

METHOD

1. Roast the flour slightly. Add salt to the flour and sprinkle a little water on it. Mix the flour with your finger tips in a circular motion till it is like grains of sago. As the grains form, remove them to another bowl. Repeat the process sprinkling water, forming granules, and removing them to another bowl.

✳

2. Tie a muslin cloth over a steamer which is three-fourth full of water. Bring water to a boil. Place the granules on the cloth, cover with a lid and steam.

✳

3. When done, spread it out to cool.
Put the jaggery, cinnamon and milk in a saucepan and heat till it is very thick. Add the cooled granules, sprinkle the sweet cumin seeds and stir till stiff. Remove the cinnamon. Spread it on a buttered dish, flatten the top smoothly and cut into diamond shaped pieces.

✳

Kiri Aluwa (Coconut Milk Toffee)

INGREDIENTS

1 c coconut milk
1/4 c jaggery
8 oz sugar
2 oz cadjunuts, chopped
1/2 t vanilla essence

METHOD

1. Boil the milk, jaggery and sugar till it becomes thick in consistency. Stir continuously. When it leaves the sides of the pan, add the nuts and vanilla essence. Pour onto a greased dish and cut into pieces while it is still hot.

Sago Pudding

Serves 4

INGREDIENTS

2 oz sago
1 c water
1" piece cinnamon

❋

3 oz jaggery
1/4 c coconut milk
1/8 t salt

❋

4 oz coconut milk
a dash of salt.

❋

METHOD

1. Wash the sago and soak it in water for 15 minutes. Drain it. Put it into a saucepan. Add water and the cinnamon. Cook till the sago is thick in consistency. Remove the cinnamon.

❋

2. Add the jaggery, milk and salt. Stir constantly till it is very thick. Pour into a wet bowl. Cool it.

❋

3. Serve with freshly made thick coconut milk and a dash of salt.

❋

Baked Vatalappan

Serves 6-8

INGREDIENTS

4 eggs
8 oz jaggery
1 pint coconut milk or cow's milk
1 t nutmeg
2 t vanilla essence
1/4 t rum essence
1/4 t cloves

✳

METHOD

1. Whisk the eggs. Add it to the rest of the ingredients and heat very gently to mix the eggs well. Do not boil, or the eggs will curdle.

✳

2. Cool a little. Whisk in a food processor, or use an egg beater. Bake at 400°F for half an hour. Switch off the oven and keep the pudding in it for another half an hour.

✳

This is a lighter version of vatalappan.

Steamed Vatalappan

INGREDIENTS

5 eggs
8 oz jaggery
1 1/4 c coconut milk
1/2 t nutmeg
1/2 t cinnamon
1/4 t cloves, powdered
1/4 t cardamons, crushed

❋

1/4-1/2 c cadjunuts

❋

METHOD

1. Beat the eggs well. Add the rest of the ingredients. Pour into a greased mould and steam for about one and a quarter hours or till it is firm.

❋

2. Serve in a mould with slivered nuts sprinkled on top.

❋

Divul Kiri (Woodapple Cream)

Serves 3-4

INGREDIENTS

1 large ripe wood apple
3 1/2–4 oz jaggery
3/4 c coconut milk or cow's milk
1/4 t salt

METHOD

1. Crack the fruit in two and scrape out the pulp, seed and all. Put them in your food processor together with the rest of the ingredients and blend for 10 seconds. Strain through a sieve. Refrigerate to cool it if you like.

   Cow's milk is all right, but the coconut milk is the best. Add a little boiled water if you prefer it less thick. It is now ready to serve. A little chilling in the fridge is nice.

   This dessert can be frozen for future use.

Banana Fritters a La Sri Lanka

INGREDIENTS

4 oz wheat flour
1/2 t salt
1 egg
1/4 pint milk

✳

some ripe sour bananas
oil for deep frying

✳

kitul treacle

✳

METHOD

1. Whip the milk and egg together. Add to the flour and salt. Smoothen.

2. Sour bananas (ambul) are the best. Peel and cut into four pieces per banana. First cut lengthwise into two, then the halves into two breathwise. Dip into the batter and deep fry in oil. Drain well.

✳

3. Put on a serving plate and lavishly pour kitul treacle on them.
Fried banana can be frozen. Reheat in a pan or oven, and then pour the treacle on them. They need not be refried, so as to avoid too much oiliness.

✳

Any treacle can be used. Even maple syrup.

Ambarella Preserve

INGREDIENTS

1/2 lb ambarella

❋

1/2 lb sugar
2 oz water
1" piece cinnamon
rose essence

METHOD

1. Peel the fruit, prick it well with a fork and put it in a bowl of cold water. When the entire fruit has been pricked, squeeze out the water and weigh it.

❋

2. Bring the sugar and water to a boil. Add the fruit and cinnamon. Boil till the syrup is thick and the fruit is translucent. Add a few drops of the essence (or rose water) and take off the fire. Remove the cinnamon.

An easy way to test if the syrup is ready is to put a bit of it into cold water. It should set to the needed consistency at once. Do not let it set too hard; when cold, it will be like a rock.

❋

This fruit is good for diabetes.

Pineapple Preserve

INGREDIENTS

1/2 lb pineapple

6 oz sugar
1" piece cinnamon
lime juice—optional

❋

METHOD

1. Cut the pineapple in half breathwise and grate it with a coconut scraper (like grating coconut).

2. Weigh the fruit. Boil it with the sugar and cinnamon until thick in consistency. Test in cold water; it must not be too hard. Add a dash of lime juice, if you like. Remove the cinnamon before bottling.

Fruit Salad

4 oz per serving

INGREDIENTS

1/2 ripe pineapple
1/2 ripe papaya
1-2 ripe mangoes
1 banana

1 apple
1/4 c cherries
1/4 c nuts
1/4 c sultanas

❋

METHOD

1. Cut all the fruits into desired sizes and mix . There is no need of sugar. Add the banana just before serving.

❋

2. One or all ingredients can be added but it is not essential.

❋

COOL DRINKS

Iced Coffee

INGREDIENTS

1 oz Nescafe
4 pint hot water
1 tin Milkmaid or condensed milk
6 oz sugar
2 1/2 t bottle vanilla essence
1 1/2 t almond essence
1 1/2 t brandy

✳

METHOD

1. Dissolve Nescafe in one pint of hot water.
   Then add the remaining water, milk,
   sugar and flavourings. Chill thoroughly.

✳

In a country that has many teetotallers, iced coffee is an elegant alternative.

Ginger Beer

INGREDIENTS

4 oz raw ginger

6 pint water

1/2 lb sugar
4 oz chopped ginger
4 oz lime juice

METHOD

1. Finely chop the ginger.

2. Boil water in a saucepan. (Do not use an aluminium pan)

3. Remove from the fire and add the sugar, ginger and lime juice.
   Cover the saucepan and infuse for 8 hours. Strain and bottle. Can be left in a refrigerator for 2 weeks.
   Do not reboil.